THE BELL AND THE BLACKBIRD

BOOKS BY DAVID WHYTE

POETRY

Songs for Coming Home
Where Many Rivers Meet
Fire in the Earth
The House of Belonging
Everything is Waiting for You
River Flow: New & Selected Poems
Pilgrim
The Sea in You:
Twenty Poems of Requited and Unrequited Love

PROSE

The Heart Aroused:
Poetry and the Preservation of the Soul
in Corporate America

Crossing the Unknown Sea:
Work as a Pilgrimage of Identity

The Three Marriages:
Reimagining Work, Self and Relationship

Consolations:
The Solace, Nourishment and Underlying Meaning
of Everyday Words

THE BELL
and
THE BLACKBIRD

Poems by DAVID WHYTE

MANY RIVERS PRESS

LANGLEY, WASHINGTON

Many Rivers Press
PO Box 868
Langley, WA 98260
USA

ISBN 978-1-932887-47-1

Library of Congress Control Number 2018939048

1st Printing: 2018

FOR

GAYLE KAREN KHO YOUNG WHYTE

WITH LOVE

CONTENTS

CONTENTS *(continued)*

CONTENTS *(continued)*

CONTENTS *(continued)*

[I]

COME WITH ME NOW

LOUGH INAGH

Come with me now,
along the
Western Way,
into deepest
Connemara,
through the valley
of the shadow,
not of death,
but of
the unconquerable
kingdom of life
we call Lough Inagh.

O love.
There is a door
beneath everything
you'll walk right by
if you don't stop to look
with that troubled heart
and a loving eye.

Come with me now
under the clouds
and skies
that sail each day
from the ocean,
under the stone-light
of the mist-wreathed
tops, through
all the streams
of falling water

and all the shadowed
mountains
we've given the name
of Connemara.

O love.
There is a door
beneath everything
we'll walk right by
if we don't stop to look
with our troubled hearts
and a loving eye.

Come with me now,
along the
beckoning path,
silvered in mist
toward
the glimmering lake,
bring every grief
you have not said
and every tear
you have not shed
and every
sorrow you've
carried alone.

There is a door
beneath everything
we'll walk right by

if we don't stop to look
with our troubled hearts
and a loving eye.

We'll arrive
in the song light
of evening
at the house
that stands
by the water,
watching
the wild geese
returning
all the length
of the shadowed lake.

There is a door
beneath everything
we'll walk right by
if we don't stop to look
with our troubled hearts
and a loving eye.

Come with me now,
on the path
that leads
to a tender
understanding,
walk beside me
on the beckoning way,

let the sun
and its rays
fall over your
shoulder
and the lake
respond
in kind,
filling your face
with reflected
light.

O love.
There is a door
beneath everything
we'll walk right by
if we don't stop to look
with our troubled hearts
and a loving eye.

We'll arrive
in the song light
of evening
at the house of light
that stands by the lake
to find the welcome
we've always wanted,
and the way we've wanted
to follow to find it,
and beyond everything,

the faces we never
believed we'd find
in the end.

O love.
There is a door
beneath everything
we'll walk right by
if we don't stop to look
with our troubled hearts
and a loving eye.

Come with me now,
along the
Western Way,
into deepest
Connemara,
through the valley
of the shadow,
not of death,
but of
the unconquerable
kingdom of life,
we call Lough Inagh.

[II]

JUST BEYOND YOURSELF

JUST BEYOND YOURSELF

Just beyond
yourself.

It's where
you need
to be.

Half a step
into
self-forgetting
and the rest
restored
by what
you'll meet.

There is a road
always beckoning.

When you see
the two sides
of it
closing together
at that far horizon
and deep in
the foundations
of your own
heart
at exactly
the same
time,

that's how
you know
it's the road
you
have
to follow.

That's how
you know
it's where
you
have
to go.

That's how
you know
you have
to go.

That's
how you know.

Just beyond
yourself,
it's
where you
need to be.

THE BELL AND THE BLACKBIRD

The sound
of a bell
still reverberating,

or a blackbird
calling
from a corner
of the
field.

Asking you
to wake
into this life
or inviting you
deeper
to one that waits.

Either way
takes courage,
either way wants you
to be nothing
but that self that
is no self at all,
wants you to walk
to the place
where you find
you already know
how to give
every last thing
away.

The approach
that is also
the meeting
itself,
without any
meeting
at all.

That radiance
you have always
carried with you
as you walk
both alone
and completely
accompanied
in friendship
by every corner
of the world
crying
Allelujah.

TWICE BLESSED

So that I stopped
there
and looked
into the waters
seeing not only
my reflected face
but the great sky
that framed
my lonely figure
and after a moment
I lifted my hands
and then my eyes
and I allowed myself
to be astonished
by the great
everywhere
calling to me
like an old
and unspoken
invitation,
made new
by the sun
and the spring,
and the cloud
and the light,
like something
both
calling to me
and radiating

from where I stood,
as if I could
understand
everything
I had been given
and everything ever
taken from me,
as if I could be
everything I have ever
learned
and everything
I could ever know,
as if I knew
both the way I had come
and, secretly,
the way
underneath
I was still
promised to go,
brought together,
like this, with the
unyielding ground
and the symmetry
of the moving sky,
caught in still waters.

Someone I have been,
and someone
I am just,
about to become,

something I am
and will be forever,
the sheer generosity
of being loved
through loving:
the miracle reflection
of a twice blessed life.

CLEAVE

To hold together and to split apart
at one and the same time,
like the shock of being born,
breathing in this world
while lamenting for the one we've left.

No one needs to tell us
we are already on our onward way,
no one has to remind us
of our everyday and intimate
embrace
with disappearance.

We were born saying goodbye
to what we love,
we were born
in a beautiful reluctance
to be here,
not quite ready
to breathe in this new world,
we are here and we are almost not,
we are present while still not
wanting to admit we have arrived.

Not quite arrived in our minds
yet always arriving in the body,
always growing older
while trying to grow younger,
always in the act

of catching up,
of saying hello
or saying goodbye
finding strangely,
in each new and imagined future
the still-lived memory
of our previous life.

MUCH HAS BEEN SAID

Much has been said about the eternal
and untouchable nature of love,
its tidal ungovernable forces
and its emergence from far beyond
the ordinary, but love may find
its fullest, most imagined
and most courageous form
when it leaves the abstractions
and safety of the timeless
and the untrammeled
to make its promises
amidst the fears, vulnerabilities,
and disappearances of our difficult,
touchable and time bound world.

To love and to witness love
in the face of possible loss
and to find the mystery of love's
promise in the shadow of that loss,
in the shadow of the ordinary
and in the shadow of our own inevitable
disappearance may be where the eternal
source of all our origins stands
in awe of the full consequences
of everything it has set in motion.

A MIND SHAPED BY MOORLAND

I am not afraid
of strange
beckonings,
flitting and unknown
horizons,
and all
the hidden ways
that fill this world.

I am not afraid
to risk myself
and be lost,
I am not afraid
to be seen
to walk into the mist
and reappear
in some other place
than first
you saw me.

Having grown
with a mind
shaped by
moorland
I am not afraid
to find my outline
made invisible
and then just
as suddenly
revealed
against
a broader sky.

I am not afraid,
of rolling cloud
and skies
half hidden
by darkness,
I am not afraid
of the cold
western wind.

I am not afraid
that I do not know,
that I cannot know,
that I cannot predict
where or what
or how,
when or where
I will appear
or disappear.

I am not afraid
of the stranger
on the cliff edge path,
walking steadily
toward me,
I am not ashamed
to tell him
or you
that I cannot
tell you,
when or where
I will arrive.

I grew
on these moors
walking
the no man's land
between east and west,
I was drawn
day after day
to horizons
that were
never the horizon
you sought
but one curve
leading to another.

I grew into journeys
that were
from childhood
always beyond
any beginning
I thought
I had made,
and any
gain of distance
I had gained,
a passage
through mist
a sojourn
in shadowed
subjectivity,
a straining to see,
a steady, growing,

continual
almost
finding out.

And the place to see
not this place
but some other place
just about
to be reached, no self
but the self
about to become
by arriving
where all along
you did not know
you had
wanted to go.

And beauty
was never a beauty
to be found
close up
never a beauty
imprisoned
by a false, touchable
recognition
but the far free
beauty of a distance
yet to be traversed,
a context
always

untouched by
any other context,
a life left alone
to reveal itself
through an almost
knowing,
an unveiling through
cloud.

Moorland
and mist
taught
me what
it might be like
to be free.

Moorland and mist
taught me
how to be
untrammeled,
to be merciful
about making
any kind
of fixed identity,
to move
forward only
like the steps
a mind might take
through
cloud thought.

Moorland
and mist
taught me
to savour
the experience
of a ghosted,
step by step,
almost arriving
on a summit
that is no summit
at all,
just a sloping
never ending,
coming to know,
holding you up
above any smaller
sense of self,
that sudden tear
in the clouds
a gift
given for a moment,
a touching of all
other moments
and all distances
the land and the rivers
and the patchwork
of fields
spreading beneath,
glorious
to the ends
of the earth.

[III]

BLESSINGS

&

PRAYERS

EASTER BLESSING

(For John O'Donohue)

The blessing of the morning light to you,
may it find you even in your invisible
appearances, may you be seen to have risen
from some other place you know and have known
in the darkness and that carries all you need.
May you see what is hidden in you
as a place of hospitality and shadowed shelter,
may that hidden darkness be your gift to give,
may you hold that shadow to the light
and the silence of that shelter to the word of the light,
may you join all of your previous disappearances
with this new appearance, this new morning,
this being seen again, new and newly alive.

BLESSING FOR THE LIGHT

I thank you, light, again,
for helping me to find
the outline of my daughter's face,
I thank you light, for the subtle way
your merest touch gives shape
to such things I could
only learn to love
through your delicate instruction,
and I thank you, this morning
waking again,
most intimately and secretly
for your visible invisibility,
the way you make me look
at the face of the world
so that everything, becomes
an eye to everything else
and so that strangely,
I also see myself being seen,
so that I can be born again
in that sight, so that
I can have this one other way
along with every other way,
to know that I am here.

BLESSING FOR SOUND

I thank you,
for the smallest sound,
for the way my ears open
even before my eyes,
as if to remember
the way everything began
with an original, vibrant, note,
and I thank you for this
everyday original music,
always being rehearsed
always being played,
always being remembered
as something new
and arriving, a tram line
below in the city street,
gull cries, or a ship's horn
in the distant harbour,
so that in waking I hear voices
even where there is no voice
and invitations where
there is no invitation
so that I can wake with you
by the ocean, in summer
or in the deepest seemingly
quietest winter,
and be with you
so that I can hear you
even with my eyes closed,
even with my heart closed,
even before I fully wake.

BLESSING FOR DIFFERENT SOUNDS

Above all, I thank you
for your many orchestrations,
for the skitter of a mouse
moving through the silent house,
or the might of waters
falling on distant shores,
I give thanks that I can hear
every form of your voice,
so that I have learned
through the years
not only the intimacy
of approaching footfall,
not only the child's cry
wanting other arms
but I have learned
to love even your warnings,
whispered or called out loud,
I have learned to live between
them, for them and through them,
through all your different forms,
and you, you have always arrived
to find me at the center,
waiting for your calm voice
of distant stars
so that my ears have learned
to live in anticipation
and to understand themselves
as the focus of arriving waves
from far beyond me

so that even in that spacious music
we call silence
I am still waiting here
to decipher your ancient language,
I am still here waiting
to hear for the first time,
the new song you have given me,
out of the origin of time itself
to find the future granted
and given back,
to listen in the silence
with the private ear created
by every separate voice.

PRAYER FOR AN INVITATION

I pray for you, world
to come and find me,
to see me and recognize me
and beckon me out,
to call me
even when I lose
the ability to call on
you who have searched
so long for me.

I pray to understand
the stranger inside me
who will emerge in the end
to take your gift.

I pray for the world
to find me
in its own wise way.

I pray to be wanted
and needed
by those I have
learned to love
and those
I must learn to love.

I pray to be wanted
and needed
by those I cannot

recognize
in my self-imposed
aloneness.

And
I pray to be wanted
and needed
by those
I wish to be wanted by.

But I acknowledge
the power
of your beautiful
disguise, and I ask
for the patient heart
of all things
to understand
the abiding
fear I feel
in following your hidden
and beckoning way,
in my
fear of receiving,
in taking your hand
to follow
its hidden,
difficult
and forever beckoning
way.

BLESSING FOR UNREQUITED LOVE

A blessing on the eyes that do not see me as I wish.
A blessing to the ears that can never hear the far inward
footfall of my own shy heart. Blessings to the life
in you that will live without me, to the open door
that now and forever takes you away from me,
blessings to the path that you follow alone and blessings
to the path that awaits you, joining with another.

A blessing for the way you will not know me
in the years to come, and with it, a blind outstretched
blessing of my hands on anything or anyone
that cannot ever come to know me fully as I am,
and therefore, a blessing even then, for the way I will
never fully know myself, above all, the deepest, kindest
wishes of my own hidden and untrammeled heart
for what you had to hide from me in you. Let me be
generous enough and large enough and brave enough
to say goodbye to you without any understanding,
to let you go into your own understanding,
to live fully in your understanding, and to gift
your understanding. May you always be
in the sweet, central, hidden shadow of my memory
without needing to know - who you were when
you first came - who you were when you stayed -
and who you will become in your freedom now
that you have passed through my life and gone.

PRAYER FOR JAMES MONAHAN

When you walked with us across the limestone,
you leaned into a parallel we could not sense,
your understanding always migrating like a breeze
across the mountain where ours could not.
Free as the air in that realm, you were bound
in this one by our inability to move fully with you,
not recognizing, not hearing, not feeling
what you felt so clearly, except in whispers,
except at the edge of things, except at the very
limit of an untouched intuition, those invisible
and urgent voices that made your everyday
so far from ours, and left you, in your well-peopled
solitude, so wondrously, so essentially, alone.

Always, always, you saw where we did not,
listened where we heard nothing, saw where
we walked almost blind, took hidden paths
we could not follow, your senses rose as if
on lark wings, or submerged themselves
in souterrains, you saw seas spreading
under mountains on some subterranean
shoreline far beneath our unsuspecting feet,
the spectrum of your sight far beyond
our mortal grasp, you were a full, turning
planetary sphere in your own heaven of understanding,
a constellation of some other collective gravity,
while we stayed four square in that flat circle
of sure knowledge we try to fathom as a human life.
Above all, you saw that great wave of revelation
coming and going like a tide off the mountain,
you saw agency and annunciation in the shadow

of a passing hawk, at the spring of knowing
called the Seven Streams, you divined a multitude
beneath our feet, saw beneath the rock, the deep
and hidden geography where Lon's people
still live and breathe, not as the dead,
but bursting with message and fresh
with news from the riven ground.

We walked along with you as you spoke
but by some divine stricture you were made
to walk so singular in your seeing, so alone
in your hearing on this earth, so alone
in your aloneness, the sheer memory of it
makes us lonely for you now as we walk,
so alone ourselves and so sorry at your going.

But one gifted, miraculous thing from your going,
now, it seems our mortal doubt, our inability to see
is healed by the simple memory of your invisible witness.
In your going we seem to have been granted
your surety of sight, so that before, where we saw
only one thing, now, when we speak of you,
we see many, where we trod alone we find ourselves,
as we recall your memory, walking with crowds
of the remembered dead and talk amongst ourselves
companionably of what you saw and heard,
as if everything you saw was occurring now,
an everyday occurrence on the mountain,
like the way in walking, we might note a passing hawk
flash by or hear the horse beat on a high meadow.

Your original, remembered, healing nobility of purpose
is so bereft of question now, so readily understood,
that we who imagine you here in some other parallel,
and who knew and loved your anxious wish to share
with us your vision, feel sure to chance a prayer
that you are happy now and still stand with us
on this same mountain, in good and knowing company,
and that somehow you have been met, and recognized
and welcomed home, and that when they greeted you,
the first thing out of their otherworldly mouths
might have been this, that you had missed one
thing and one thing only in your precious sight,
and that was the simple knowledge that you were
never alone, neither amongst your mortal loved ones,
nor your bereft friends, nor the ones who waited
on the other side of all your singular belief.
And that all, all, was healed and forgiven
by that single, clear understanding given to you now.

A prayer for you then, James Monahan,
for this world and the next, with your healing hands
and your generously rendered heart, from all of us
who embrace you in their memory and their
understanding,
and in the true spirit of your visionary sight.

A prayer for those who might have met you
in your too-soon arrival in their realm,
their strong, receiving arms around your shoulders,
their eyes and ears hearing at last into your hearing

and seeing so deeply into your seeing,
looking together with you at the earthly paradise
where you always knew you made your mortal home,
seeing with you, every wonder you ever knew,
every ordinary, extraordinary corner
of the blessed world you tried to show us,
all of them laughing and pointing
with you, all along the mountain,
anointing your sight with their vision,
everything as true in their eyes now,
as it ever was in yours.

BLESSING FOR ONE WHO HAS TAKEN
THEIR OWN LIFE

You decided to leave us
but we can never leave you,
not in our minds,
not in the inner
recess of our
wondering hearts,
nor in the long twilight
horizon where you
will always walk
in our memory.

Above on the mountain
the lark will rise
from the summer grass
to the sky above your home
and the song it sings
will forever carry
the mystery
of your going.

You turned away
from all our help,
so that we have to
ask for your help
now, not in answers
but in asking
all the difficult
and beautiful
questions your life
bequeathed.

You never asked for
the helping hand,
but still we hold
our hands out now
to take yours in ours,
to reassure you
in the quiet of the morning
or the silence of the night
and in all the days
to come
when in our minds
you still need our care
to help you go on
where we can't go,
to see you safe
beyond the quiet line
of our understanding,
to walk with you now
arm in arm
with our regrets
and our affection
that one last mile
along the way you
wanted to go, the quiet
in which we wave
goodbye, only the sign
of our secret promise
to you, the continued
and helpless testament
of our unspoken love.

[IV]

WINTER GRIEFS

WINTER GRIEF

When you find
yourself alone
in this winter's
narrow light,

when you want
to come out
of the darkness
only to confirm
you can
return
there again.

When you see
by a single glance
through
the misted window
that the rain
has come to beat
on your
walls.

When you watch
yourself alone
and walking,
when you watch
yourself alone
and remembering
so closely
what you never
wanted to remember.

When everything
near to you
is too near to you
and everything
faraway,
is still too far away.

Let this wind
and this winter
and this rain
and this weather
and all
the difficult blessings
of the world
find you here,
walking
in the
shelter
of white walls
under the tracery
of stone windows
in the nest
of greenness
at the valley floor
below
a sailing sky
between mountains
and green fields
among centuries
of the rested dead.

Let the green
that laps at their graves
hold your memories
in place
when they want to slip
through your hands.

Let the rest
in this rested place
rest for you.

Let the birds sing
and the geese call
and the sky race
from west to east
when you cannot raise
a wing to fly.

Let evening
trace your loss
in the stonework
against a fading sky.

So that
you can give up
and give in
and be given back to,
so that you can let
winter
come and live

fully inside you,
so that
you can
retrace
the loving path
of heartbreak
that brought you here.

So you can cry alone
and be alone
so you can let
yourself alone
to be lost,
so you can
let the one
you have lost
alone, so that
you can let
the one
you have lost
have their
own life
and even
their own
death
without you.

So the world
and everyone
who has ever lived

and ever died
can come and go
as they please.

So you can
let yourself
not know, what
not knowing
means.

So that
you can be
even more generous
in your letting go
than they
were
in their leaving.

So that you can
let winter
be winter.

So that you can let
the world alone
to think of spring.

GOODBYE FOR NOW

(For John O'Donohue)

After the storm, and the sideways bluster of the rain,
after you had opened the door in the falling light
and stood upright in the shelter of the dripping thatch,
after the goodbye and the tears and the turning away,
there was that far, horizontal, ocean gleam across
the threshold of the West as if keeping the dark at bay,
a last farewell after your Wake, not a closing but an
invitation, not a last light but a glimmer of a meeting to be,
something that had happened before and would happen
again, seen now in the light of your going as the sheer,
miracle and gifted ordinariness of evening light, something
I realized you were now wondering at through my eyes,
something we were now seeing together from that invisible
foundation that waits on the other side of sadness,
something that had once been shared and would be again,
and then from the bright falling nowhere in the center
of the dying sun, a risen thought, almost spoken
between us, *goodbye for now,* and you, raising your hand
as if you'd see me again, making a way through the waves
and the sea-light, and the distant miles, into the west.

MAAM CROSS

(For John O'Donohue)

You've felt it before,
a cold blustery,
pitch black night
on the road
to Maam Cross,
the headlights
sweeping the
moorland edge
of something almost
apprehended,
not quite glimpsed,
the appearance
and disappearance
of things half at the edge
of memory
half on the brink
of becoming real.

And the flutter
in the chest,
that memory
of you
once here,
now gone,
on this same road
sitting with me
as we looked
with almost

the self-same eyes
and thoughts,
a witness
to all the appearances
and disappearances
of the way ahead,
the mist coming
and going
as it always did
over the Bogland
by your home,
while the night outside
held its breath,
waiting for morning
and the dawn glitter
of the new day,
but for now,
we drive in a form
of half-lit
mutual forgiveness
me forgiving you
for going,
you forgiving
me
for being still alive
in all this
continuing wonder,
the conversation
half real, and half not,
just like the days
after your going.

Both of us
in that old male way
looking forward
and away into the distance
even as we speak
to each other
in all three tenses at once,
past, present and future,
a future we are still
in some ways
finding together
driving on,
as we will now forever,
of a winter's night
following this long stretch
of misted unfamiliar,
familiar road.

AVIGNON ELEGY

(For John O'Donohue)

The invisible conversation you held while you
were alive can still be heard in every quiet sun
shadowed wall, in the birdsong of morning, and
in the last light of evening, the final rays above
the river drawing the shape you make in the air
by your absence. So that even in the warmth of
the southern night I hear your laughter singing
from the same familiar sunlit nowhere you always
inhabited even before you left and that still flows
with us, morning or evening, invisibly close to
where I go.

Even in narrow streets, surrounded by stone, I
listen through those walls in parallels now, and at
times inhabit a third body where I seem to hear an
unseen heart beating close to mine, counting the
seconds of my life, as if telling me to live fully in
this parallel until I come, some fateful day and meet
you, standing at the threshold of yours.

When I speak, the words are no longer mine to
give away, even though I begin alone, we seem to
finish every sentence together and often in ways
I needed but could not imagine, so that now I
cannot tell where I begin a theme and you join in,
and I wander among my friends, wondering if they
know to whom they speak.

I know now our friendship led us somewhere
beyond ourselves because the impetus of your death
continually leads me to places where I feel you just
about to appear again, your hands lifted toward me,
as they were to everyone, your laughter reminding
me of what I wanted while you lived and breathed,
your body strangely reborn in mine, and yet
continually coming and going from me, at times
the familiar line of your back suddenly turning
to that shouted wave at the corner before you
disappear; off to some imaginative otherness where
others wait, but always returning after an hour, a
day a month, a year, the beckoning stranger come
to meet me, shaking hands as if for the first time,
the light in your eyes alive again to another future,
chosen again, with no shadow of parting.

ORPHAN LAMB

A black lamb centered in a green field,
his thin breathed-into sides confirming
his bereft call for milk amongst the bedraggled
white fleeced mothers, looking on,

who stood and watched, not hearing
'plaintive' or 'lost' or 'waiting to be fed'
but the cry of another mother's son
needing to find his own way back

to the flow-source of milk and the warm
fleece hug of his mother's belly
swaying above the teat. They would stand
above his black skeletal form beneath the trees

dropping their heads to drive him off
and stamp and turn again, nudging their own
half hesitant, half happy lambs away.
We walked the fields an hour looking

for a mother standing alone or with a single lamb,
the burnt sun falling to a misted light,
the trees become silhouettes, black as the lamb itself,
our eyes and ears in the crowded field

bent to the ancient prayer rising around us,
the evensong of grief and motherhood,
call and response, wanting and not wanting,
the church bell call of a passing rook
sounding the hour as the last pale
just burnt gold of a cloud framed

our shadows, walking the lit vale
toward the car, toward loss, toward

something in our low disappointed voices
trying to remember from childhood both
the sense of source and the act of being pushed away,
where we were wanted and where we were not.

In the end, we took him home, to a waiting mother
who had lost her own, penned in a barn,
her grown head turned away in the wooden crush
so the lamb could drink and hours later

in the sweet hay strewn dark of the enclosing barn
the mother ewe could smell her own milk
tasted through the lamb's own breath
their mutual life come to life by self-recognition,

the black lamb pulling mightily at the dugs
as the mother looked on, as we looked on,
and looked at one another
passing the tiny airline bottle,
the faint breath of whisky from our nip
misting and pluming in the half-lit barn.

The single, full malt taste of something met,
a breathing through in the chest, a way of coming to
and of tasting again, the essence of wanting to live,
something paid for by our seeking and our patience,
just a tang, a hint, a mere breath in the glow light,
of being born again.

WOUND

(For Dougie Whyte)

The young broken life
waking for a moment
on a clean white pillow,
the blood at the corner
of his mouth like a red twig,
now broken
against the healing linen
and the light from
the high window
on the side of his face
as if come from far
away and arriving
from a distant loving nurse,
while beneath his chest
the raw hollow
where the front of his stomach
makes a wall of bandage
and somewhere under it all
the rough pasture of dull ache
and sharp stone
he walks in his mind
where his wound has become
the place he is open
to a future now
disappearing
now appearing
as something
he is being asked
to recognize

more like a past
going forward
than a future
come back to him
suddenly
close to his mother
and father
and the brother
and three sisters
and the fields
around the house
where he used to run
with friends
and where he goes now
his breath stopped
but run free
like the lines
on his cheek
and like the soft
somber half light
falling like rain
on his upturned
face.

THE ACT OF LEAVING

I must have wanted
to take this road
of sack cloth and ashes
walking my way to
a quiet aloneness.

I must have wanted
to leave the light
of those eyes
and walk into
the dark,
I must have wanted
not just to find
another,
but the need
to find another.

I must have needed
to disappear
from what I knew
and loved
so I couldn't be found
by the same eyes
or heard by the same ears,
I must have wanted
to have my heart broken
by being found
in a different way,

I must have wanted
to whisper my way
into another
conversation
with another horizon,
to be heard
by other ears,

and be seen
in another light
and joined to another
world.

I must have wanted
to feel
the pain
of departure
and the distress
and the
heartache
and
I must
have intuited
all along
that first glimmer
on the other
side of sadness.

Looking back
at it all
it is almost
impossible
to believe,
that I stood
in the full
necessity
of that grief.

That I had faith
in what
I wanted,
that
I must have
wanted
what I wanted.

[V]

MUSE

AN ALMOST

An almost,
a something
just beyond me,
a swerve in the light,
and a passing blur
like a peregrine
from a cliff edge,
sometimes a darkness,
a pushing away,
a not wanting,
often a digging in,
a head down
concentration working
against a coal face
of nothing,
a breathing close
and at the same time
a fight for breath.

Many times, a someone
I do not recognize,
a wondering if,
a hand in mine,
pulling me on,
above all, an invitation,
and always in the end
a lovely and difficult surprise,
like silk torn in two,
a rested view from
a high window,

passion followed
by real love,
and like love,
an edge and then
the willingness
for the necessary
but as yet
unannounced
sacrifice.

Always a death,
the passing by
of a grave
on the way
to somewhere else,
my hat dipping
slowly in calm respect,
above the grave
birdsong,
yes, happy birdsong,
then not birdsong,
mourning,
an annunciation
not quite heard,
a frontier
deep in the chest;
most of all,

being called
a sense of great migration
a needing to leave,
a wanting to cross.
Then, that good day,
standing on the threshold
between this world
and the next,
like the crest of a pass,
and the path
going over, through cloud,
about to descend
to the promised land,
the flurry of wind telling me
I'm about to free myself
of an upward way,
my vision a notch in the sky
opening wide,
and above the lark song
filling the living, breathing world,
with its own anticipation,
its own way of looking back
at me, and through me,
and like me, always
found in a new light,
always ready to be
wanted again.

CLOSE COMPANION

Close companion
of my work
often unseen
at the surface
married
at the center.

Two lovers
now forever
in troth
to the future
we make
by being
entwined.

Wings
of the dove
never seen,
whose beats
keep
everything
on the wing,
migrating
between
silence
and speech,

I follow you
silently,
never speaking
always
speaking
of you.

I turn
to the open
page
like a lover's arms
always finding
you there
when I look
long enough,
when
I invite
deeply
enough,
when
I lift my pen
and rend
my heart
at the possibility
of your going.

HOMAGE

(For Mary Oliver)

So simple
so clear,
so here.

Like a cat
pawing
the air
or the whip
crack
sound
of a dog
snapping
at a fly.

Always
toward
the end,
the way
we are never
quite
prepared
to find
the beautiful
sense
of hidden
pleasurable
and complete
surprise

in the poem
until
reading
the
very
last line,

but which
is
the one
you
remember
and
that stays
with you
day after day
when you do.

[VI]

SEEING YOU

A GIFT OF TIME

(On Giving the Gift of a Watch)

The timeless beauty of your face, looking by stealth
can see again the beckoning face of time itself,
can witness both time and the timeless in one gold face,
never counting our hours together as one heart,
but counting every single one we spend apart.

BOW

Seeing you
place that stone
so carefully
on the roadside
shrine,
I inclined my head
to watch it
balance and stay
as you
lifted your hand
so breathlessly
away,
just the slightest
most subtle
inclination
of the head
toward
you,
that afterwards
walking
toward evening
I realized
had been
my bow.

SEEING YOU

I want you
to see
yourself
the way
I sometimes
see you.

I want you
to see
yourself
with the
self-same
eyes
that have me
shy
of telling you
what I see.

I want you
to come across
your self
and see
yourself,
the way I did
that first
morning,
as a beautiful
incredibly
kind
and inviting
stranger.

I want you
to knock
gently on
your
own door
and stand
there
astonished
as I do
unable
to speak
to the one
who has come
out to meet you.

Like Rilke's
visiting
angel
of the
Annunciation
who forgot
his message
to Mary,
and could only
fall back
to singing
her praises,

stuttering and
overwhelmed
as he was,
by the untroubled
beauty
of her soul.

EVERLASTING

Between waves, under the moon's light
after the passing of your smile into memory
when the last silence falls and your voice
is no longer heard over the shadows
of the earth, when even the rain has stopped
and my memory and my words and my arms
and my hands that held you have fallen away
with the tide of time, retreating forever
into the beckoning everlasting dark;
when everything we know has gone,
when my heart has stopped and yours
no longer calls to mine through the distance
of our time together – others will live in this life
and this love and this light, that we have set
in motion, so that underneath that far off,
yet to arrive and sheltering darkness,
underneath the deep and almost touchable nearness
of all things, underneath the breath of our words
joining together for this privileged time of times,
they will see in the distant pinprick stars
the returning light of the dawn we made together,
as we live in the light and the love of those
who came before us, and who helped us to see
and celebrate and recognize ourselves
and who brought us here and whose light
we now pass on, so that even at the end
of time, even in what looks like silence,
even in the quietest sense of disappearance,
even in the far distance of times beyond
our present understanding, we will be remembered
in the way others still live, and still live on, in our love.

DREAM

In the dream, I am living in some indeterminate
time delineated only by the late atmosphere
of the sky at dusk, a house alone in the mountains
and my moving silhouette sharp against the moorland
light, happy at the end of a working day in some
old northern landscape, rearing sheep and walking,
with two tired, panting dogs at my side, to a lighted kitchen,
the last embers of the fire brought to life by my kneeling.
But one thing remains the same in this abstraction,
when I look over my shoulder and smile, you are there
to greet me, to take my hand and walk with me
in the last of the precious light, talking together
of some future that cannot be imagined even by my ideal.
Our love of dreaming together as good as any future arrival.

NEWLY MARRIED

Awake at midnight
in the darkened
house,
I look up
at the full, bright
white circle
of the moon
and walk aglow
in the pale light,
the frost outside
a perfect reflected
snow of whiteness
edging
my lifted hands,
against the spreading
night, my pointed finger
following, through
a window pane,
a single glittering
star adrift
in a vault
of the black sky,
while around me
the moonlight
paints every single wall
a shade
of silvered white,
outlining
the dark, moving center
of the silhouette
I call a self.

In a life defined
by difficult
passages
I am that
rare tidal
hardly ever
experienced thing,
a walking
glowing, undefined
lamp of anticipatory
happiness, looking
over the roof tops
of an unsuspecting world,
a disturbing
effervescent unarticulated
someone who has
promised something
he has promised
to reflect on
and live through
and come to understand.

Beneath the covers
I hear her
silent breathing
like an unspoken
vow to the luminous
circle of all the seasons,
to the coming and going
of breath and memory,

to the spring before
we knew each other,
to the end of the moist
Irish summer
when we first had met,
and then to that
Italian October
still living in our cells,
when we walked
in Florence
among the
falling leaves.

One thing
I have learned.

How difficult
it is to die
from my
disbelief
and kneel
down
to the truer
underlying
font of happiness
waiting to
break
the enclosing
surface,

to believe
in my body
that
I deserve
the full spacious
sense of
not being
thirsty anymore,
of living
a present
contentment.

But this spacious
season,
this cold winter night,
following a mid-winter
wedding,
under the pale white
moon
or the frosted sun,
I am strangely
in the midst
of this happiness,
full of memories
of past happiness,
as if I could hold
each epoch
in my
hands again.

I am full
of clear forgiveness
to what clouded
that happiness
and I am careful
and alert to what
is needed to
keep our present
joy.

I am a groom
to the possibility
my vows expressed
and my hands
and my arms
and my speech
and my thoughts
are shaped
to the care
of that possibility.

She sleeps
and I walk
under the moon
close to her
breath and her body,
not wanting
to wake her,
wanting to wake

and reach for
her sleeping hand
under the covers
to feel that slowly
curling palm
in mine telling me
this happiness is
unutterably ancient,
living at a rested
eternal center
where I have allowed
myself
to come to ground,
and fall
all at the same time,
which is after all
not only
a foundation
and a falling toward
the other,
but toward
a shared future
never experienced
before,
to become real
on both the inside
and the outside
in the company of another
and I realize

as I take her hand
under the moonlight,
that I have been
newly
married all my life,
courting the
morning
hours since
childhood,
down on my knees
to the possibilities
of the day,
alert, in the ferry line
off the island,
to every
pilgrim possibility
of travel,
committed fully
to the next view
along the road,
to the beckoning
horizon
of everything
that appears
and disappears,
like the
miracle touch
of this palm in mine,
so physical,

so real,
this frosted
silver
evanescent night
amidst
all the
grievous
vanishing.

I want to open
the doors
to the garden
and stride out
into the quiet
neighbourhood,
knocking on doors
and waking everyone
from their own quiet
romance with sleep,
shouting,
I am a man
in
love with
possibility,
and most
especially,
most intimately
most surprisingly,
as they stand

there in their
pyjamed
surprise,
wondering
at their
previously sane
neighbor,
now pointing
at the
frosted upstairs
windows
of our nearby house,
with that one particular
form of possibility
sleeping so quietly,
so unsuspectingly,
so companionably,
so warmly
beneath
the moonlit sheets.

[VII]

TRAVELS

AUSTRALIA

The light has come to find you again, even on the far
side of the waking world, look inland and you catch
the dark interior core of what only looks like an empty
centre, look outward and you see the tidal run of ocean
stretching forever from the shore on which you stand,
above all and across both, newness and the unimaginably
ancient, singing together, and then everywhere, light
painted on light, in the sky, on the ground and in the faces
of those looking not at you but through you,
to the beckoning horizon, to the pale night of a southern
sapphire sky, or even beneath you, through the dust
of the endless earth, to the dream-time in the mind's eye
of what has happened and what is about to happen,
even in the crowded cities, even on the endless coast,
even in the beautiful interior desolations that never grew
a single tree. We feel it when we hear the growing whisper
of rain feeding the parched ground, or in the inward growth
that makes what has been hidden begin to show its face
in the world, the unspoken sense, not of being free now,
but the anticipation of being allowed into something deeper,
further, beyond our living in the everyday, into the beckoning
endless land, into the blue-hilled horizon, into the oceans'
mounting roar, an unspoken and indescribable freedom
just about to happen, reaching for that fatal shore, we sight
only the edge of this waiting land, riding forever, the slow,
curling, but never breaking wave of our longed-for arrival.

TRACKING

(for Marius Swart)

We walk
as shadows
in the shadow
of the trees,
black against
the green and gold,
the ochre roads
shading into distance,
the red stone
kopjes above
standing
in morning light,
like noble profiles
of silent witness.

We cradle
as temporary
our sense
of distance
edging closer,
as we track
the spoor
of a preoccupied,
wandering,
elephant snapping
branches beyond
the limit
of our human
ears.

Your confident
shadow
leading us quietly
through
the twilight veldt
teaches us
that what is real
is only
what is
just about
to happen,
what is gift
has not yet
been given,
that
a true sense
of being is
our ready
anticipation
to see
and be witness
to what lies beyond
us, like an
overwhelming
everyday
sense of presence
we must follow
and face
and fully discern,
like a newly
discovered shadow
always working

forward
of our present
understanding,
something
just on the edge
of appearance,
and something we are
forever trying
to track
and now,
as we close,
something
actually here,
a held-backness,
a massive, gentle
almost reluctant
dangerousness,
always, even
as we close
upon it,
just beyond
our seeing,
just beyond
our
knowing,
even as we finally
imagine we
catch it,
at the very edge
of sight,
ghosting
through trees.

[VIII]

NAKASENDO

RIVER FALL

We follow
the river's fall
down through
the mountains
all day, but now
our bodies
have stopped
to rest,
the water still flows on
without us.

FOREST PATH

The white
forest path
that brought
us here,
and a kettle
just boiled,
our tired eyes
warmed
by the steam
from
lifted cups.

AFTER WALKING

After walking
in the heat
to Tsugamo, the cool
evening light
on the Ryokan
ceiling makes every
memory clear.

SHOJI

In the moonlight
of the early hours,
a shadow across
our shoji window,
a hesitation, a shout.

Someone else
stumbling
toward home.

ONE EAR

After the heat,
my head resting
on a cool
buckwheat pillow,
one ear listening
to the river.

SLEEP

Closing my eyes,
the body seems to fall
and to follow
the same waters
it followed all day,
tumbling
through darkness.

ECLIPSE

The moonlight
on your breast
suddenly eclipsed
by a shadowed,
loving hand.

FOOTSTEPS

Walking
through pines
and birdsong
this morning,
thinking of Basho.

Who will walk
in my footsteps?

MIST

White wisps
of clouds on the mountain
quietly reaching down
when we
looked away, to cover
the path
that brought
us here.

OLD FRIENDS

The clouds,
the blowing rain,
and the clear
bent mountain pine
against the sky:
three old friends
who never had a dime,
still helping
each other,
after all these years.

THE BAG ON MY BACK

The bag on my back
is full of presents,
my head
with memories,
my feet with every
step I've trod
along the way.

THE PASS

The pass was always
just over the next
rise of trees,
a notch in the skyline.

One day I will take
my last breath
from that
beckoning sky.

⌈ IX ⌉

IRELAND

OGHAM

There were words hidden in the wood
I could not read, the black lines incised
by some careful hand long gone, the rise of a moon,
or the hidden note of a harp struck along the charred edge,
a notation able to carry the ancient hysteria
of battle or the way a woman's face
can console, destroy or embolden;
then in my reverie of the spaced lines, a sudden direct
hearing and a seeing, the harsh grate of the heron
in a following wind, the half memory of a traveler
seen through a door, calling for bread through
the gusted smell of ash and fire-smoke,
the words spoken back from the edge of the wand
both welcome and warning,
the past like a taste, a spell, an incantation;
the familiar, inspired hesitation in the lines
of notched hazel, both imagined and absolute.

RUAN

A touch of earth, a falling between things, a red berry
from a bent rowan, rolled in the palm then crushed
and put to the mouth, a wave-taste of the next world
growing stronger, Anu arriving in silver, her bent lips
brushing the forehead of the one anointed to hear.

Thus the listener was given the fullness of revelation
next to his ear, thus the dawn spread of light was placed
in his mouth, and all of us stood in respect, as he rose
equal to the morning, the deer shadowed in mist,
the breath at the back of the morning greyness,
and from the first miracle of that far in-light,
a world created from newly opened eyes.

STONE

The face in the stone is a mirror looking into you.
You have gazed at the moving waters
you have seen the slow light, in the sky
above Lough Inagh, beneath you, streams have flowed,
and rivers of earth have moved beneath your feet,
but you have never looked into the immovability
of stone like this, the way it holds you, gives you
not a way forward but a doorway in, staunches
your need to leave, becomes faithful by going nowhere
something that wants you to stay here and look back,
be weathered by what comes to you, like the way you too
have travelled from so far away to be here, once reluctant
and now as solid and as here and as willing
to be touched as everything you have found.

FINTAN

The pool near Slane where hazel brushes the gleam of water
and the just ripe nut touches and un-touches the still
cold darkness of a shaded stream, the wet
encircled shell a meniscus of light for the rising mouth
of a silvered salmon, scale and sleek. The moon,
the wait, the strike, the plash of dawn-lit water,
whoever ate this fish that fed on the tree of life,
whoever caught and cooked and then consumed
the flesh of the messenger god, would make no king,
would uncover no gold to hoard against the coming awe,
would become mortal-wise through words enfleshed
with the nut of truth, would become equal to the task,
of living and dying, a man acknowledged,
as one who could now speak for others, who would now
speak for others, greatest of poets in a land of poets.

WRAITHS

The shadow of tree-fall, the winter frosted darkness
of an iced woodland pool edged by white, the un-light
deeper than the inner eye could travel, we passed
over the whitened ground knowing we were seen
clearly from the other side as we approached.

In silence, we walked, one after the other
in single line carrying the weighted, deep respect,
our teacher taught us; remembering to hold our heads
with the nobility of promise he held so well
when that night on the mountain, he led us
through the door of fear and dread, schooling
our minds with silence repeating precise
yet beautiful questions we were taught to ask
when caught in the presence
of powers beyond our mortal thought.

That shared dedication brought us here,
and told us that the threshold had been reached,
we were taught after all to be alert to omens
others would walk by: we were taught to know
when the stricken wound in time was touched:
to watch, as if from afar our own body swoon
as if struck by the world's accumulated grief,
so that when the frost-rimed bracken cracked
beneath us, when we walked as if on the threshold
of another world, when the ground seemed
to give way and rear up, we heard the vixen scream
within us without fear, but still listened to its cry
aware that day was night, pretending to be day,

and still went on walking deeper in toward them
listening in our heart-source for the whispered
voice of he who had thought us equal to this task,
reminding us to bless the souls of those who had spent
their days swimming from darkness to light
and back never knowing their way; who
wanted help from we who they most frightened.

And so, as we were taught, we called on aid
and assurance from those others who had traveled
before so surely from this world to the next, and so it was,
as our chant began, that we saw them, passing swiftly
over the frozen ground, haunting the dark mist robe
in which they were swathed, their sorrowful faces
turned toward us as if to invite us to grief like some
beautiful home we had always wanted but not yet found,
beckoning us through their dance of fateful disappointment.

We stood unmoved and approached then, like stern
but loving parents, clear we were equal to the quest
and saw in their grief-filled eyes that it was too late
for them to avert the blessing we had brought,
like an inverse of death, killing them back to life
and we stood four square before them,
holding the walls of their fear at bay while they beat
with their voices at the outer edges of our attentive love
trying to break it down, refusing to believe,
but crying in the end, that they could not leave
their pale palace of disappointment where they
had haunted and hated and feasted on absence.

In the silence that followed their dissolution
we released them all to another life,
and thus we saw the mist robe fall,
heard cries drift and disappear against
the linen grey of birch bark,
saw the invisible pearl of each snowdrop
become something else briefly in their undoing
as they fell and nourished the warming ground,
felt spring breathe in our smiling mouths,
turned outward again to a future newly emboldened
by our powers and in the aftermath, saw every
miraculous thing as if originated by love;
looked shyly into one another's eyes
seeing our teacher had taught us well,
and through the outlined shadow of the trees
spreading with new leaves, saw the new morning
as a simple burst of sun through spring rain.

THE COMING OF AMERGIN

The first sign, a twist of foam, scattered
and weed wracked, drawn back by the pull
of gravel and water, then the beach scoured
by green and the thump and turn of the first wave
foretelling his arrival, then deer running ashore,
out of the waves, foam-scut become stag's
horn, curved and white in the mist-break
of morning, making for the inland woods,
some other flood breaking behind them,
and after that, the white wave flight
of a hawk rising, clutching, as it flew, a silvered
writhing salmon, caught in its claws,
then the thump and long retreat again
before some wave vibration under the water,
the far-off call of something summoned,
the fear-break of creatures cornered
in a burning depth, caught and flung
toward us in a roar of wind, the rising wall
behind it curved into the hard tusk of a boar
made white and sharp against a blood red sea,
the mad hog shouldering past us in a gale of wind.

Then, a foaming, breaking wave-form,
into which we looked waiting for his coming
as our hair first streamed behind us
then fell limp in the back and run of wind
and water, and the shivered light gave way to silence.

We felt then, the slow closing grip of hands
at our necks like those of a quiet ghost, telling us
our breath of life in this land had gone out,
our time was done and out of our own mouths
came the first whisper of a future that condemned
us to the underground, each cry an intuition
of exile, an utterance like a sharp skin cut, salted,
wind-scoured and cold, and in the receding water,
a full going back, an almost never coming back,
followed by silence, a pause in the world beat,
as the sun rose sharp behind the coming figure,
and through the ninth wave no outward arrival,
but an inward surge, a roar on the inside,
a glimpse of our life in the other world, looking back
at this life from the other side of a question
we had never wished to ask, condemned
to the dark while his life and the life of his people
became manifest in our lighted world,
and so the island became his, and his people's,
while our world-door shut fast, they triumphed
so that now we must look for a way to be undefeated.

My final memory of that day, the way
his triumph was marked by the final
unwanted miracle; the dying of wind
that allowed him ashore.

THE MIRACLE ISLAND

(Inishbofin)

Two lads really, two young men, half hidden between
waves, crested then hiding, hiding then cresting, rowed
their Curragh on the rolling ocean, their heads
and their dark shoulders appearing and disappearing
as they looked over that gently breaking green garden
of white flowers we call a wave, to see a silvered calf,
lit and grazing, nuzzling the foam amidst a gleam of waves.

Rowing and turning to look, rowing and turning to look,
their lithe black Curragh swam through the summer haze
until they rocked in a whisper, near to the byre heat of its
glittering hide, under the shadow of its marvelous light,
a helpless witness to unheeding beauty, drifting in silence
they circled its slow moving, immaculate whiteness,
cropping the water.

Then, they hesitated, they leant, they balanced
in the swaying cradle of the waves, wanting to touch,
unable to touch, until one graciously, generously
and silently leant the other way, while the other
reached out, brushing gently the sea-silk
of its untouched whiteness.

Feeling the feather of that tremulous hand,
the calf half turned to look, and held them both steadily
with the knowledge of its eye, half in sorrow
and half it almost seemed, in some knowing gladness
at being caught at last and they found themselves

looking back, not knowing what to do or say
until beneath them the Curragh hung for a moment,
reared up solid, and grated softly to a rapt stillness.

When they turned to look, the calf was gone
but the island stretched before them like a wave,
headland after headland, its bays leaping with fish,
its green pastures calling like mothers
for a calf of their own and all around them,
the familiar gull cries, the smell of Dulse
and sea moss, the waves giving up their
once distant lives, on that hushed, receiving sand.

And from then on, the miracle was remembered
and told like this, not in the unheeding beauty
of the glittering calf, nor in the astonishing appearances
or disappearances of our tidal world,
but that on the first sight of the island
that they had come to know, through every fibre
of their being, and in the very depth
of their hearts and through every future exile,
what it felt like to have found a home.

LEAVING THE ISLAND

(Inishbofin)

It must be have been
the slant of the light,
the sheer cross-grain of rain
against the summer sun,
the way the island appeared
gifted, out of the gleam
and the depth of distance,
so that when you turned
to look again,
the scend of the sea
had carried you on,
under the headland
and into the waiting harbour.

And after the pilgrim lanes,
and the ruined chapel,
the lads singing beneath the window,
and the Corn-Crake calling from
a corner of a field,
after the gull cries and the sea-hush
at the back of the island,
it was the way, standing still
or looking out,
walking or even talking
with others in the evening bar,
holding your drink
and laughing with the rest,
that you realized–part of you
had already dropped to its knees,
to pray, to sing, to look–

to fall in love with everything
and everyone again, that someone
from deep inside you had come out
into the sea-light to raise its hands
and forgive everyone in your short life
you thought you hadn't, and that all along
you had been singing your quiet way
through the rosary of silence
that held their names.

Above all, the way afterwards,
you thought you had left the island
but hadn't, the way you knew
you had gone somewhere
into the shimmering light
and come out again on the tide
as you knew you had to,
as someone who would return
and live in the world again,
a man granted just a glimpse,
a woman granted just a glimpse,
some one half a shade braver,
a standing silhouette in the stern,
holding the rail,
riding the long waves back,
ready for the exile we call a home.